FISH

Other titles in the series
Keeping and Caring for Your Pet

Guinea Pigs: Keeping and Caring for Your Pet
Library Edition ISBN 978-0-7660-4184-4
Paperback ISBN 978-1-4644-0299-9

Kittens: Keeping and Caring for Your Pet
Library Edition ISBN 978-0-7660-4186-8
Paperback ISBN 978-1-4644-0303-3

Puppies: Keeping and Caring for Your Pet
Library Edition ISBN 978-0-7660-4187-5
Paperback ISBN 978-1-4644-0305-7

Rabbits: Keeping and Caring for Your Pet
Library Edition ISBN 978-0-7660-4183-7
Paperback ISBN 978-1-4644-0297-5

FISH

Keeping and Caring for Your Pet

Angela Beck

E **Enslow Publishers, Inc.**
40 Industrial Road
Box 398
Berkeley Heights, NJ 07922
USA

http://www.enslow.com

Contents

1

Preparation and Setup   7

Where Fish Feel Most at Home
Fascinating Aquariums   8

Before You Begin
Planning and Preparing   10

Useful Tools
Technical Equipment   12

Fish-Friendly Living Conditions
Setting Up Your Aquarium   14

Here We Go
Using the Aquarium   16

EXTRA
Quick Solutions for Water Problems   18

At a Glance
My Care Plan   20

3

Fish and Plants   39

Tetras   40

Carp   44

Catfish   48

Labyrinth Fish   50

Live-Bearing Tooth Carp   52

Killifish, Halfbeaks   54

Cichlids   55

EXTRA
Advice on Fish Diseases   60

EXTRA
Types of Plants   62

At a Glance
Aquarium Care When
You Go on Vacation   68

2

Plants and Maintenance   23

The Right Environment for Fish
Water and Water Care   24

Other Important Factors
Temperature and Oxygen Content   26

Green Oasis
Aquarium Plants   28

Fish Friends
Correctly Choosing Your Aquarium Fish   30

Healthy Diet
Feeding Your Fish   32

EXTRA
Quick Solutions to Plant Problems   34

At a Glance
Adding Fish to Your Tank   36

Copyright   70

Index   71

Further Reading
(Books and Internet Addresses)   72

1

Preparation and Setup

Fascinating Aquariums   8

Planning and Preparing   10

Technical Equipment   12

Setting Up Your Aquarium   14

Using the Aquarium   16

EXTRA
Quick Solutions for
Water Problems   18

At a Glance
My Care Plan   20

Fascinating Aquariums

Most of us would love to have a glimpse into the mysterious underwater world of the Amazon or a river in the Thai jungle or perhaps Lake Tanganyika or Lake Malawi in Africa. . . . An aquarium is a great way to realize this dream within your own four walls. Keeping an aquarium is a fascinating hobby, which will teach you many new things.

Fish Habitats

To keep a successful aquarium you will need to know how to care properly for your fish and plants. The best way to do this is to make the aquarium environment as close to the natural habitat of your fish as possible. All of your fish originate

from the tropics and have settled into a variety of habitats, from the smallest pond to the sea, from bubbling springs to sometimes rushing, sometimes sluggish streams that lead to a huge river with a strong current making its way to the broad delta of the sea.

Due to varying rainy and dry seasons, the living conditions of fish change throughout the year in a particular rhythm. These changes include water chemistry (elements and pH), physical factors (water temperature, changes in air pressure, different water levels), and also lighting conditions. Depending on the mineral source—for example, the bed or bank of a river—the water can be soft, acidic, and low in nutrients, or it can be hard, alkaline, and nutrient-rich. The color may be red to dark brown (black water) or crystal clear (clear water) to grayish (white water). The picture on page 24 depicts the contrast between black and white water in Brazil. The process of evolution has ensured the best fish have adapted to the different conditions. They live well but not always in the land of plenty, and sometimes their food supply is very low.

Many fish habitats are in danger of being destroyed.

Mimicking Nature

Compared to the vastness of tropical environments, an aquarium is a mere thimble of water. The conditions in the aquarium must be just right so that the fish and plants can thrive and even breed. However, the more extreme the type of water in which the fish live in nature, the more knowledge is needed to keep these fish.

Beginners

If you are keeping an aquarium of fish for the first time, it is best to choose species that originate from the tropics but have adapted to different environments. Even though these types of fish originate from Southeast Asia, the water conditions in which they now survive are much easier to recreate in your home.

Conservation

Some aquarium fish species are able to thrive better in tanks than in their original habitats because of pollution and other environmental threats. Most aquarium fish these days have been bred in an aquarium and are not taken straight from their natural habitat. In order to create humane conditions for the fish in your aquarium, you will need to consider which types of fish and plants you want to keep together. Then decide on the type of aquarium, its features, and, most importantly of all, the correct type of water.

The Thailand onion plant grows vigorously in its natural environment (pictured above).

Planning and Preparing

Shopping List

- [ ] tank with insulation
- [ ] cabinet
- [ ] tank cover with lighting device
- [ ] fluorescent tubes
- [ ] background
- [ ] filters, filter equipment
- [ ] heating, thermometer
- [ ] glass cleaner
- [ ] plastic tubing for water changes
- [ ] suction device for cleaning
- [ ] gravel
- [ ] decorations (roots, rocks, clay pipes, etc.)
- [ ] ground fertilizer
- [ ] water treatment products
- [ ] start-up bacteria
- [ ] water test kit (nitrite, pH, KH)
- [ ] CO_2 permanent test
- [ ] CO_2 pressure regulator
- [ ] aquatic plants
- [ ] fish food
- [ ] fishnet
- [ ] no fish ... yet!

The first step to a beautiful aquarium is to visit a pet shop, where you will find a large selection of healthy fish and plants. Here you can seek expert advice on fish as well as the right equipment.

So-called bargains, such as used or homemade aquariums, are a bad idea. A faulty tank without warranty, inadequate technology, or obsolete equipment can mean a disastrous end to a new hobby and will not provide optimal growth conditions for fish and plants.

In an Apartment

Check with your landlord whether it would be all right to keep an aquarium. As long as the tank does not damage the home, it should not be a problem.

Insurance

It is a good idea to ask your parents about updating their liability insurance so that any damages caused by an aquarium will be covered. Water damage can be expensive. Check that your floor can take the weight of a tank containing about 40 gallons of water. The necessary information can be obtained from your landlord or architect. The total weight of the tank will be about two pounds per quart of water, plus the weight of the tank itself and the surrounding cabinet.

Where to Put It?

The best place is in a dark corner of the room because direct sunlight promotes the growth of algae and will heat up the water. Do not place it on a windowsill or next to a window. Another good reason to keep it in a dark place is that the scenery will look more beautiful when lit up from behind. Smaller tanks are best kept on a desk or stable wall shelf. Or how about an aquarium as a room divider?

Stable and Balanced

The tank should be stable and level. If necessary, adjust the balance of the surrounding cabinet.

Tip

You will not need to worry too much about stability if you buy a tank with a surrounding cabinet. It will need to be near a power supply and four outlets.

The Tank

Choose the largest tank possible because a large tank looks better, is more biologically stable, and is easier to maintain. In addition to the standard rectangle shape, you can buy triangular and octagon-shaped tanks as well. Some have beveled or curved fronts, which add a whole new dimension.

Best Place for the Heater — Tip

Make sure the heater is free of gravel or decorations, and place it opposite the filter inlet. Carefully pull out the electrical plug whenever you need to change the water in the tank.

→ Tank Size

20 x 12 x 12 in = 15 gal
30 x 12 x 12 in = 20 gal
24 x 12 x 20 in = 25 gal
48 x 12 x 16 in = 40 gal
36 x 18 x 19 in = 50 gal
36 x 18 x 24 in = 65 gal

Well-Heated

Because most aquarium fish originate from the tropics, they need to live in warm water. There are several types of heaters available for your tank. The most common is controlled by a thermostat. Select the correct wattage for the tank volume and the room temperature. As a rule, for a room temperature of 68°F, a heat output of 0.5 watts per quart of water is required. For a room temperature of below 68°F, you will need 0.75 watts per quart. If the fish require more than 78°F, choose a heater that emits one watt per quart of water. The heating should not be too strong, however, or there will be a risk of overheating if there is a problem with the thermostat.

Floor Heating and Thermal Filter

If you want even temperatures, lush plant growth, and complete safety, a floor heating system with heating cables and accurate electronic temperature control is what you need. Thermal filters are also very practical; they filter the water and control the thermostatic temperature at the same time.

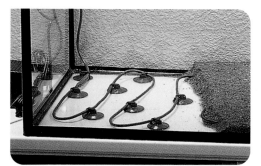

Accurate Measurement: Aquarium Thermometer

Monitor the temperature with a good aquarium thermometer. The best system to have is a plug-in thermometer as well as a dockable floating thermometer.

This type of thermometer will measure the water temperature accurately.

Technical Equipment

The Filter

The purpose of the filter in your aquarium is to remove excess food, decaying organic matter, free-floating particulates, dangerous chemicals, and the fish's waste products from the water. The fish excrete waste constantly as they swim around in the water. If this waste is not removed, the toxins that the fish are excreting from their systems will rapidly build up in the water and poison them. Early stages of this are called ammonia stress. When it becomes fatal, it is ammonia poisoning. In addition, particulates floating in the water and decaying food and other organic matter can contribute to cloudy aquarium water if not kept in check.

Size and volume of the filter depend on the tank size and type. It should be suitable for the needs of your fish. Every hour, the filter cleans 80 to 100 percent of the tank contents. Air-pump filters are ideal for tanks of up to sixteen gallons. This type of filter can help maintain the right amount of bacteria in the tank. Suction and water movement are useful for mixing up the tank's contents. Also suitable are electronically adjustable internal filter modules. External filters and thermo filters are suited to very large tanks, as is a trickle filter. Modern aquarium filters are energy efficient, easy to use, and silent and have precise technology and beautiful design. Make sure you buy one with a guarantee and safety mark.

Filter Materials

Mechanical filter equipment helps remove solid waste particles from the water. Filter materials include synthetic cotton, mesh, fleece, trickling filters, clay pipes, and foams filters, which contain good bacteria that help break down harmful substances, such as nitrites and ammonia, found in the tank. For the biological breakdown of any harmful substances in the water, you will need a trickling filter or a special substrate filter, which draws water down and through the elevated substrate in the aquarium. Substrate is what you put at the bottom of the tank—for example, gravel, sand, or peat.

Before you can add the fish, it usually takes two to three weeks to filter the tank water completely. This time can be greatly reduced by adding start-up bacteria. Change any dirty filter material once you notice the filter is not working as well as it should be. For harmful substances, such

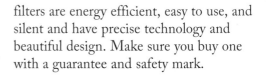

Keep Some Bacteria   Tip

Do not change or clean all of the filter material at once so there are always enough bacteria present.

as chlorine or other chemicals, or to remove any yellowness of the water, you can also use a carbon filter. Carbon filtering is commonly used for water purification and in air purifiers. Carbon filters are most effective at removing chlorine, sediment, and volatile organic compounds (VOCs) from water. They are not effective at removing minerals, salts, and dissolved inorganic compounds.

Chemical filters are useful when the water chemistry needs altering—for example, using a peat filter for acidification. Chemical filters quickly clean the water and use a diffuser to enrich the oxygen in the water.

Ventilation

If you have a well-planted aquarium with only a few fish, ventilation may not be required. If the water gets too warm during heating periods, it can lead to

oxygen deficiency. Air-powered vents should be used at night, when the plants consume oxygen, and they should switch on and off automatically by a controlled timer. Some gravel filters also come with ventilation pumps.

Light

Light is vital for good plant growth and the well-being of the fish and many micro-organisms. For example, fish need light for their skeletal structure (vitamin D3 synthesis), skin, metabolism, and general health. Choose a tank cover with a light reflector and multiple fluorescent tubes. You will need 1.6 to 2.8 watts per gallon of water and one tube per four inches of depth of water. The combination of several light colors (to make up the spectrum and therefore emulate sunlight) is the most favorable for plant growth. LED aquarium lights with a high proportion of blue regulate verticle growth, and warm-tone lamps with a high proportion of red encourage growth width-wise. HQL lamps are best for open-top tanks.

With the help of different technologies, you can create fish-friendly living conditions.

Some plants grow out of open-top tanks.

Setting Up Your Aquarium

The correct aquarium equipment will help keep your fish healthy. You will also need plants for decoration so that your aquarium resembles a vivid natural habitat. Clean the tank inside and outside thoroughly with vinegar, rinse it off, and dry it before filling it. Check that it sits on an even surface by using a bubble level. For thermal insulation, insert an insulating board or mat underneath the tank that is about one-quarter to half an inch thick. If the tank is kept in a cool room, do not forget to insulate the sides as well.

The Background

An aquarium background provides more depth and makes your aquarium look nicer. For smaller aquariums, you could use a photo background showing a calm, natural-looking scene, which attaches to the outside of the tank. If you want more depth, thermoformed back panels painted with patina create the most natural scene. (Patina is the bluish green film that forms on copper—for example, the Statue of Liberty or an old penny.) The tank needs to be pushed right up against the back wall for the best effect. You can also place a simple frame behind the tank.

Neon tetras thrive in densely planted and well-designed aquariums.

Other Equipment

Place Styrofoam™ tiles under large rocks or rock structures. Next, install the technical accessories, such as filters, heaters, and the CO_2 pressure regulator, but do not start them up just yet.

The Correct Substrate

Substrate is the material you line the bottom of the tank with. For lush plant growth, you will need calcareous (made up of calcium carbonate) aquarium gravel with a grain size of about one-eighth to a quarter of an inch. Anything else will be harmful for the fish. The gravel should be as rounded as possible (not sharp!) and colored with a special paint. Before you fill the tank, you will need to wash the gravel thoroughly. If you want to keep armored catfish, you will need to fill one-third of the floor area (front or middle part) with round gravel (1 to 2 millimeters in grain size) about 1.25 inches high. Otherwise, you will need a layer of gravel about one-half to three-quarters of an inch high. Then on top of the gravel, evenly spread a slow-release fertilizer containing iron and then cover it with another 1.25 to 2 inches of gravel. The level of gravel should increase toward the back of the tank. This makes the tank look nicer and also makes it easier to remove waste products.

Roots, Stones, and Hidey-Holes

Many fish need roots (e.g., catfish need them for grazing) and stones to hide behind. Suitable stones are basalt, granite, noncalcareous shale, or stone timber. All roots from the pet store should be sandblasted and be as strong as possible. Soak them until they sink in the water.

The level of gravel should slightly increase toward the back.

Fresh wood from the forest will not work because it rots and floats. Also soak any fish furniture made of clay or brown beech leaves before use. Place these in plant-free open spaces. For fish that have babies in the gravel or use the gravel as a habitat (for example, killifish), add fine sand and peat fibers to the substrate to make it cozier. For Lake Malawi and Tanganyika tanks, lime-pit stones work best.

The background can either be put in the tank or attached to the back.

Make It Fun

Sketch a planting plan to help you decide where to put plants, roots, and stones. Use the nature and aquarium photos in this book to inspire your creativity. The most important thing is that your aquarium meets the needs of your fish.

Here We Go
Using the Aquarium

Fill With Water

Fill one-third of the tank with warm water, approximately 73°F, using a watering can with a fine spray. So that nothing gets stirred up, pour the water slowly over a deep dish. Once all aquatic plants are in the right place, fill the aquarium carefully to about three-quarters of an inch below the tank's edge.

Run the Water

Fresh tap water can be dangerous to fish and plants because it contains harmful chemicals, such as chlorine and copper, especially early in the morning. Therefore, it is wise to use a water treatment, available from pet shops, to neutralize these substances. If your tap water is too hard, meaning it has too many minerals in it, it will need to be softened (see page 19). Some pet shops sell softened water. To ensure the water conditions are right, use start-up bacteria to break down toxic substances (see page 12). This shortens the waiting period considerably, so the water will be ready for your fish sooner.

Turn On and Tune In

Then add your devices (filters, heating, etc.) to the tank. After three to four hours, check that all devices are functioning properly. It is a good idea to put the lighting on a timer that comes on at 9 A.M. or 10 A.M. and stays on for about ten to twelve hours.

Only put the fish in the tank when no more nitrite is detectable and the nitrate content is below 40 ppm (parts per million or milligrams per liter).

Safety Tests

There are many different tests you can use to check the safety of the water. Depending on the kind of fish you are keeping and what their natural habitat is like, you may have to purchase a CO_2 permanent test and kits that measure levels of pH, ammonia, nitrates, nitrite, calcium, water hardness, and other factors. First, fill a test tube with water from your aquarium. Then, add special chemicals into the test tube with a dropper. After the water and chemicals mix, it will turn a color. Next, compare the color in the test tube against a chart. Different colors

Aquarium Safety

- → Check the location and stability of the aquarium cabinet.
- → Check for the guarantee and safety mark.
- → Fit a safety fuse before switching on the power supply (this interrupts the power in case of any electrical faults).
- → Unplug all appliances before cleaning the aquarium!
- → Install a check valve behind the air pump and CO_2 pressure regulator.
- → Check tube connections and the filter on a regular basis.
- → Clean silicone tubes with cotton wool.

Healthy, flourishing plants will make your aquarium look good.

indicate different levels of the item you are testing for. Read the instructions included in the kits very carefully. There are also electronic monitors that read the levels of chemicals and elements in your aquarium water. These are more expensive than regular kits.

→ *Aquarium Information*

Size/volume:

Setup date:

Filter type:

Fertilization system:

Tube type:

Next tube change on:

First fish added to tank on:

Fish species:

Fish purchased at:

Person who sold the fish:

Quick Solutions for Water Problems

→ The Most Common Water Problems

Problem	Cause	Solution
cloudy water	too many microorganisms or algae, dead fish or snails, fermenting substrate, overfeeding, overloaded filter material	Use UV-light to kill the micro-organisms and algae. Change filter material and try using a carbon filter, which can be bought from a pet shop.
gray, greasy film on the surface of the water	buildup of bacteria due to lack of surface movement	Do a partial water change and use water-treatment products. Skim off the greasy film. Set the filter so that it ripples up the water surface.
water smells musty or like something is rotting in the tank	rotting gravel, water not changed frequently enough, dirty filter material	Check the substrate and replace if necessary. Change the water frequently. Change the filter material and use a carbon filter. Regularly clean out any sludge and waste.
water is yellowish brown	too many secretions, too much tannic acid and humic substances	Do partial water changes. Check pH, nitrite, and nitrate levels regularly. Carbon filtration will remove yellowish-brown color but not all the substances.
gravel is blackish brown, foul-smelling bubbles rise up from bottom of tank to surface, plants rot from underneath, roots are black	incorrect soil composition, rotting materials (peat soil), too fine gravel, gravel layer too high interrupting water flow	Change the substrate. Gravel size needs to be 3 to 5 millimeters. The layer should be about 2.75 inches high. Use a substrate fertilizer.

Problem	Cause	Solution
snails dying	chemicals or incorrect water additives, fish are eating the snails	Check the water levels and change as needed. During any chemical treatments, remove snails and keep them separate.
water too acidic (pH too low, see page 25)	insufficient carbonate hardness, too much acidifier, too much CO_2	Do a partial water change. Aerate the water. Check the CO_2 level.
water too alkaline (pH too high, see page 25)	too much hard water, calcareous decorative material, main source water too hard	Decrease hardness to 3 dH (partial water changes using demineralized water). Use peat filter and CO_2 and if necessary, remove or test peat.
water too soft (see page 25)	insufficient carbonate hardness in water source	Do partial water changes with water of a higher alkalinity. Add water hardener, available from pet shops.
water too hard (see page 25)	tap water too hard, calcareous decoration material or filter material	Do a partial water change with deionized water or water softener. Use peat filter.
filter cover disc has hard gray layer	calcification from water due to high carbonate hardness (KH) values	Remove the filter cover disc and clean with hydrochloric acid (10–20 percent) or vinegar. Remove chalky deposits using a mechanical disc cleaner. Test KH values and correct if necessary.

My Care Plan

Daily

→ Check whether the technical equipment is working correctly, including CO_2 permanent test and CO_2 pressure regulator (air pump).

→ Check the water flow through the filter and the tube connections.

→ Feed the fish and check whether they are healthy and have an appetite.

→ Inspect the plants.

Weekly

→ Replace the tank water every one to two weeks by one-fifth to one-quarter and add a water treatment product.

→ Two days later, add a standard fertilizer (with potassium) and change the CO_2 test.

→ Every one to two weeks, test carbonate hardness, pH, iron, and oxygen, always at the same time of day.

→ Carefully clean the filter disc cover and the upper edges of the tank with 10 percent hydrochloric acid.

→ Clean filter disc covers with an algae magnet or glass-cleaning product.

→ Remove yellow leaves and any plant remains.

→ Clean the feeding ring.

Monthly

→ Measure the oxygen level (page 26), test the nitrate levels (change one-third of the water if the nitrate level is greater than 40 ppm).

→ Clean out any sludge and waste products.

→ Depending on the degree of contamination, clean a portion of the filter material with lukewarm water or replace it. Add a bacterial preparation.

→ Cut off stem plants and trim any plants that have grown too long.

→ Clear out any floating bits of plants.

→ Check CO_2 levels.

Every Now and Again

→ Clean the filter pump head every three months.

→ Replace fluorescent tubes every eight to ten months (not all tubes at once—space it out over a week).

→ Freshen up the floor of the tank once a year with fertilizer balls.

2

Plants and Maintenance

Water and Water Care   24

Temperature and
Oxygen Content   26

Aquarium Plants   28

Correctly Choosing Your
Aquarium Fish   30

Feeding Your Fish   32

EXTRA

Quick Solutions to
Plant Problems   34

At a Glance

Adding Fish to Your Tank   36

Water and Water Care

As a good solvent, water contains many dissolved substances that cannot be seen with the naked eye. In an aquarium, certain processes can take place that change the water chemistry. Only a chemical analysis of information will reveal what has actually happened. All substances in the water affect the well-being and reproductive systems of animals, plants, and microorganisms.

Natural Habitat

Aquarium fish mostly originate from tropical waters and have successfully adapted to the water conditions of their natural habitat over millions of years. Fish owners should try to create optimal living conditions in their aquariums, those of the natural habitat of the fish, so they can survive and thrive. Some flexibility is possible because, in nature, from place to place, seasonal differences in water temperature and composition occur, but any variations should not be too extreme. You can buy excellent chemical-analysis and water-treatment products from pet stores to help you keep an eye on your tank's water chemistry.

General Hardness (GH)

This is the sum of all the dissolved calcium and magnesium salts in the water; this can be determined by a GH test. General hardness can be measured in different units. We will use degrees of general hardness (dGH) in this book. The GH is made up of the water put in the tank plus substances from decorative material (gravel, coral, etc.) and the hardness buildup in the water over time. The total water hardness can be reduced by adding water from reverse osmosis or demineralization.

GH influences the condition, morbidity (how often your fish gets sick), metabolism, nerve and enzyme activity, skeletal and cell structure, and reproductive readiness of the fish. Magnesium is responsible for enzyme activation, and a deficiency of this substance leads to problems in muscle contractions and blood clotting.

During confluence (the flowing together of two or more streams or rivers), white water and black water mix very gradually.

Carbonate Hardness (KH)

This is the sum of the dissolved carbonate and bicarbonate compounds in the water and has an acid-neutralizing effect. The interaction of the KH with the pH has a strong influence on the well-being of aquatic organisms: the KH acts as a pH buffer and prevents a too strong and rapid decrease in pH, which can be deadly. KH is affected by CO_2, acids, and biogenic decalcification. KH that is at a 3 to 10 degree (dKH) level is ideal. Cichlids and Lake Malawi and Tanganyika fish need levels above 10 dKH. These values should vary by no more than 3 dKH above or below.

→ **Water Hardness**

0–7 dGH	= soft
8–14 dGH	= medium hard
15–21 dGH	= hard
above 21 dGH	= very hard

→ **pH Value**

0–6	= acidic
7	= neutral
8–14	= alkaline

pH Value

This is a measure of all acidic and alkaline substances dissolved in the water. The measure of the ion concentration (charged particles) is logarithmic—for example, a pH change of 6 to 7 is ten-fold, a change by two steps is a hundred-fold concentration change. Such huge changes can cause the fish significant discomfort or even kill them. So it is very important to keep pH levels correct according to which fish you have in your tank. A continuous CO_2 (pH) test will help keep your fish safe. Unhealthy pH values cause damage to organs, fins, and mucous membranes; problems with elimination and protein coagulation; gill burns; swimming problems; stress; disease susceptibility; and decreased fertility.

The water chemistry in your fish tank should recreate the conditions found in the natural habitat of your fish.

Other Important Factors
Temperature and Oxygen Content

Temperature

The water temperature must meet the needs of your fish. Low temperatures slow down the metabolism of cold-blooded animals and lead to death. Levels that are too high lead to stress, lower life expectancy, and reduce the oxygen content of the water. Rapid temperature changes lead to stress, darker water, agitation, increased respiration, and gas-bubble disease. Therefore, the water for your fish should be kept no more than 3.6°F above or below the recommended temperature.

Oxygen

Fish, plants, and microorganisms need oxygen to survive, which is produced by plants through photosynthesis. The oxygen content in the water is dependent on the temperature. The oxygen saturation should always be at least 80 percent of the values shown in the table below; under 50 percent will lead to such problems as listlessness, loss of appetite, restlessness, gasping, and disease susceptibility.

Lack of Oxygen

The following can cause oxygen deficiency:
→ poor-quality gravel, sludge, waste products, unkempt filters
→ too many fish, too much fish food
→ respiration of fish, respiration of plants during the night
→ lack of light, too few plants
→ algae

→ dead snails
→ oxygen depleting substances, such as chemicals added to the water
→ too high temperatures

Suggested solutions:

→ ventilation
→ partial water changes
→ prevention of harmful factors (adding products to water)
→ filter maintenance
→ more plants, better lighting

Oxygen

Use a test kit from a pet supply store to measure the oxygen content of the water in the tank. Record the result. Next, fill a graduated cylinder with water from the tank and keep it in the dark for forty-eight hours at a temperature of 77°F. Measure and record the oxygen concentration of the water in the cylinder. Compare the two values. To find out how much oxygen was lost, you can calculate the percent decrease. Subtract the second value (oxygen content of the water in the cylinder) from the first value (oxygen content of the water in the

Measuring water chemistry levels in a natural habitat

→ *Oxygen Saturation*

°F	*Maximum Saturation*
59	10.6 ppm
68	9.1 ppm
77	8.3 ppm
86	7.6 ppm
95	6.9 ppm

Healthy plant growth produces vital oxygen for your fish.

The surface of the water needs to move constantly so necessary exchanges of gas can take place.

tank). Divide the difference by the first value. You will get a decimal point. To turn the decimal point into a percentage, multiply the decimal by 100. This number is the percent decrease. A decrease of more than 20 percent of the oxygen content is cause for concern.

When to Add Your Fish

Immediately after you set up the tank, the aquarium plants are not yet fully grown, the water is often cloudy, and the water levels are not yet biologically correct. The important bacteria in the gravel, filter, and tank have not yet reached sufficient amounts in order to be able to break down any nitrogen compounds. Organic substances, such as the feces and urine of the fish, uneaten food, and dead or decomposing plants, form ammonium and ammonia. The bacteria called Nitrosomonas break ammonia down into nitrite. The bacteria Nitrobacter convert toxic nitrite to nitrate. This process requires oxygen (see diagram).

Wait about two weeks and test for nitrite. Only when the nitrite test shows no presence of nitrite can the fish be added to the tank.

Nitrates can be removed by regular partial water changes. The nitrate content should remain below 40 ppm.

Get Good Water Faster! **Tip**

You can shorten the initial waiting period by using a bacterial preparation available from pet shops and some used filter material.

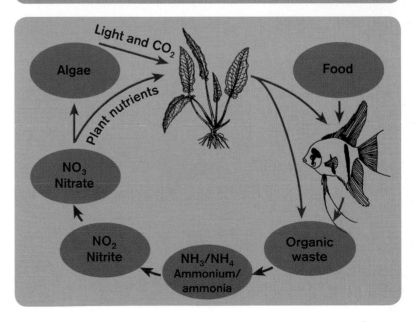

Light and CO_2

Algae

Plant nutrients

NO_3 Nitrate

NO_2 Nitrite

NH_3/NH_4 Ammonium/ ammonia

Food

Organic waste

Green Oasis
Aquarium Plants

Aquatic plants are more than just attractive decorations. As well as producing oxygen, they also improve the water quality in the aquarium. In addition, they provide a habitat, food, hiding places, and spawning grounds for your fish.

Interior Plant Design

Short, low, quick-growing plants should be in the foreground. Mid-height plants should adorn the sides and open spaces in the middle ground. Solitary plants need space to be effective. Tall plants should be put in the background.

Aquatic plants create a natural habitat.

Aquatic Plants

→ produce vital oxygen
→ detoxify the water
→ can work as antibiotics
→ recycle waste materials and break down harmful nitrogen compounds
→ have roots that keep together loose gravel
→ keep algae under control
→ serve as fish food
→ serve as hiding places and spawning substrate and provide territorial boundaries
→ provide a habitat for microbes
→ are beautiful decorative items
→ mimic natural fish habitats
→ can quickly grow and multiply

Small Groups of Plants

Put all plants in small groups together, except for the solitary plants. Arrange the plants from front to back according to their height, with short plants in front and tall plants in the back.

Preparation

Take care to choose plants that are healthy and strong-looking and remove any soil, dead leaves, and substrate (rock wool) from the pots, as well as worm eggs (jelly) and algae. Cut off any rotten stems and cut back the brown, thick roots by about one and one-quarter inches.

Planting

Make a hole in the gravel with your finger and place the roots or stems inside without crushing them. The shoots should remain above the substrate. Arrange the plants so that the leaves do not overlap. Tubers, bulbs, and rhizomes should remain one-third uncovered by gravel. Java moss and ferns and *Anubias* can be tied to a rock or piece of wood with some nylon. Do not use lead or lead wire staples because these will pollute the water.

Plant Care

Free-floating plants should only cover 10 to 20 percent of the water surface so they do not block the light required in the tank. Use them sparingly and tie them to a food ring. Any loose weeds should be taken out right away. If plants grow too tall for the tank, shorten them and rearrange the leaves to make them look nice and neat.

Plant Nutrition

There is no need to use slow-release fertilizer on a long-term basis to support your aquarium because the plants soak up nutrients from the water through their roots and leaves. However, each time you change the water, you will need to use special fertilizers (which also contain potassium) according to instructions. Iron is quickly used up, so it should be added daily (regularly check levels with an iron test kit). In addition, plants need CO_2 in gaseous form. Make sure you purchase a good-quality CO_2 pressure regulator.

In Southeast Asia, aquatic plants are grown and picked by hand.

One example featuring attractive contrasts of leaf color and structure

Water	Value of tap water	Ideal value *	Date	Date	Date
Temperature					
Carbonate hardness (KH)					
General hardness (GH)					
pH value					
Nitrite (NO_2)		0			
Nitrate (NO_3)		below 40 ppm			
Oxygen (O_2)		above 80%			
Iron (Fe)		0.1 ppm			
Phosphate (PO_4)		less than 0.1 ppm			
Carbon dioxide (CO_2)		up to 10 ppm			
* regulate according to different fish species					

Correctly Choosing Your Aquarium Fish

Your fish are the stars of your aquarium. Read on to find out exactly what your fish need so that they are able to thrive, and, in turn, give you a lot of joy.

Only a few aquarium fish are caught directly from the wild.

Proper Fish Selection

There are so many types of fish! How will you choose? When you are looking in the iridescent fish aquariums at the pet shop, you need to choose carefully and resist the urge to buy as many different types as possible. This is because not every type of fish will get along in your aquarium.

Note the following points when choosing and socializing your fish:

→ Check that each different species has the same temperature and water requirements.

→ Schooling fish feel at home in a shoal (at least six fish).

→ Only choose a few different species for each tank.

→ Do not choose fish that are likely to fight or chase other fish.

→ Some fish can only be kept individually (e.g., male Siamese fighting fish).

→ Algae-eating fish, such as armored catfish from the genus *Otocinclus* (dwarf suckermouth), are ideal to start up your tank.

→ Make sure the nutritional requirements of each species are similar.

→ Initially only buy fish that are easy to keep. If the species you want is not listed in this book, please follow recommendations from your local pet shop. In addition, see the further reading section for more information on pet fish (page 72).

→ Never overfill the aquarium with fish. As a rule of thumb, keep one inch of fish per quart of water.

The Ideal Fish Community — Tip

Before you buy your tank, or at the very latest before setting it up, you should decide which types of fish you want to keep. A randomly thrown together "aquatic community" will give you no joy in the long run. Some types of fish just do not get along well with one another because they have such different needs.

Freshwater shrimp can live together well with small fish species.

the water surface and should not sway or twist or bump into decorative materials. The feces, if you can see any, should be dark and well-formed, not gray and formless. Healthy fish should also be eager to feed when offered food by pet-shop assistants.

When Buying Fish

Make sure that the fish in the pet shop aquariums are awake and lively with spread-out swim fins. Body and fins should be free of gray, red, or bloodshot patches, injury, plaque, and small white spots. The fish should look strong (not shriveled) and completely healthy. The fish should not be gasping for air at

Aquarium Mates **Tip**

Other interesting species that live well with fish are freshwater shrimp, apple snails, and African dwarf frogs. Shrimp are particularly ideal for your fish community.

The larger the tank, the more species of fish you can have.

Feeding Your Fish

The vitality, health, color, and fertility of your fish are partly dependent on the quality and quantity of their food.

Complete Food

Scientists have developed high-quality food for aquarium fish that mimics their natural food. Commercial fish food can come in flakes, granules, or food pellets.

Bloodworms will be eagerly gobbled up by most fish.

White mosquito larvae only survive in unpolluted waters.

Water fleas make suitable live food for some larger aquarium fish.

It contains all the important nutrients your fish need. When buying fish food, make sure it is in airtight, moisture- and light-proof packaging, and it should be fed to your fish when fresh, if applicable. Good food is eaten quickly. Surface fish will swim up for it, and some food will slowly sink down (for the fish in the middle-water zone) and remain on the ground long enough so the fish on the bottom can find enough food. You can buy special food for fish offspring. Fish food and tablets should not make the water murky.

Live Food

Some carnivorous species, such as piranhas as well as some species of pike and perch, need the movement stimulus of prey, so you will need to provide them with live food. Tubifex worms are commercially available but increasingly rare because they originate from habitats that are now highly contaminated. Unfortunately, this kind of food is becoming hard to find in natural waters due to pollution.

In addition, many waters are protected from fishing, and many places frown upon or prohibit people from collecting worms or other animals used as fish food. The microscopic crustaceans Daphnia and Cyclops, also known as water fleas, are already becoming quite rare.

The larvae of phantom midges, a type of fly that looks like a mosquito, should only be fed in moderation. Black mosquito larvae provide a good source of nutrition, but they should not be allowed to mature because the adult females sting. Unfortunately, if you use live food, there is the risk that you will have uninvited guests in your tank, such as pathogens and parasites. Snails can bring tiny animals called hydras into the tank, for example.

The use of live food could cause diseases to be introduced into your tank.

Special Food

A compromise between natural live food and processed food is frozen live food. Thaw the food before feeding by putting it in a net under running water, then add liquid vitamins, which you can purchase from a pet store. Big fish love larger chunks of food. You can buy large frozen food, such as earthworms, mealworms, and crickets, from many pet shops.

How and When to Feed?

To make the most of the prey drive of your fish, you should not only provide a varied diet but also hide the food in different areas of the aquarium. The best way to do this is to use a spoon or fish feeder. In order to avoid overfeeding, only give your fish an amount they can consume within a few minutes. It is far better to feed your fish several times a day rather than giving them one big meal. It does not matter what time you feed them, but do not feed them within an hour of turning off the lights. Only crepuscular (active at twilight) and nocturnal fish will feed after you switch the tank lights off.

Food Fun

Take the time to observe your fish when they are feeding. You can buy food tablets that can be stuck on the glass wall of the tank in order to get a better glimpse of your fish community. Tablets on the bottom of the tank will encourage the normally secretive catfish as well as snails and shrimp out of their hiding places.

Tablets offer fun-foraging opportunities for your fish.

Quick Solutions to Plant Problems

→ The Most Common Plant Problems

Problem	Cause	Solution
holes in leaves	nibbled by fish or snails, possible vitamin deficiencies	Identify any pollutants. You may need to swap them for new plants. Use fertilizer. Regularly change the water to reduce high nitrate levels.
yellow plants, not growing	nutrient deficiency, too little CO_2, problem with gravel, not enough light	Use a good fertilizer. Increase the amount of CO_2. Renew fluorescent tubes over three days (after six to eight months of life, they significantly decrease in luminosity).
rotting water trumpets	excess nitrate, bacteria, suddenly changing all the fluorescent tubes at once	Do a partial water change. Use a peat filter. Use water treatment products.
leaves lying flat on the ground	incorrect light color or tube	Use lamps or tubes with stronger blue light.
stems growing excessively tall, pale or yellow in color	wrong color of light, too little light, too short a duration of illumination, too little CO_2, inadequate fertilization, iron deficiency	Optimize lighting (try using more red). Increase CO_2. Use a good fertilizer that is rich in iron.
floating plants not growing, dying	too little light, not far enough away from filter discs, dirty filter discs	Clean the filter discs. Use more light. Try opening the tank and shining a lamp into it.

Problem	Cause	Solution
plants covered in aphids	aphid-friendly environment	Remove plants for a short while. Labyrinth fish and some carp eat aphids. No chemicals!
a greasy, shimmering bluish-green layer of algae on the glass of the tank, decorative materials, or gravel	poor water condition caused by too few aquatic plants, too many fish, overfeeding, too much phosphate fertilizer, high nitrate levels, too few water changes, blue-green algae growth due to alkaline water	Clean algae off tank. Add more plants. Check the pH value and change the water if necessary. For improved oxygen content, do not overfeed your fish. Use the right mix of lighting colors and change the time of lighting. Do regular partial water changes. Change filter material regularly.
grayish brown deposits on aquatic plants and tank glass	slimy buildup of algae	Clean the surfaces of filter discs with a disc cleaner. Check luminosity of lamps and replace them if necessary. Check the nitrate levels in the water. Algae-eating fish include the Siamese algae eater, bristle-nosed catfish, and dwarf suckermouth catfish. These can be introduced for biological algae control.

Adding Fish to Your Tank

Buying Your Fish

→ Transport catfish separately because the spine on their dorsal fin could damage your other fish.

→ Ask for an opaque bag to transport your fish in to reduce any unnecessary stress for your fish. Also, cover the bag with a newspaper, for example.

→ Keep the bag warm, and get home as quickly as you can. Do not place it on a hot or cold car seat.

→ For short distances of less than forty-five minutes, if in a large bag, fish can be transported with no additional oxygen required.

→ Before putting your fish in the tank, test the transport water (KH, pH, oxygen). If there is a large difference between that and the tank water, get your fish used to the new water very slowly and in small steps.

→ Get a clean bucket and soft net.

→ Open the bag and add approximately one-fourth of a quart of your tank water.

→ Cover the tank lights or switch them off.

→ Place the bag in the tank, and leave it there for about fifteen minutes (pin it to the edge using clothespins) so the fish can adjust to the water temperature.

→ Then pour half the water from the bag into the bucket, and refill the bag with tank water.

→ After another fifteen minutes, place the net over the bucket, gently pour the contents of the bag into the net, and then put your fish in the tank. Pour out the water from the bucket.

→ Watch your fish, but leave them in peace. Switch on the lights the next day, and feed them.

→ For newly bought fish or fish that need special care as well as any baby fish, keep a separate tank ready.

→ In case of illness, always get an accurate diagnosis and, if necessary, consult a veterinarian.

→ Follow any medication instructions exactly as written.

→ Sick fish must be treated in separate tanks. Remove any dead fish with a net, and clean the net with boiling water.

→ After each use of medication in the tank, use a carbon filter. Remove after three days, do a partial water change, and then add fertilizer and start-up bacteria.

Fish and Plants

Tetras 40

Carp 44

Catfish 48

Labyrinth Fish 50

Live-Bearing Tooth Carp 52

Killifish, Halfbeaks 54

Cichlids 55

EXTRA

Advice on Fish Diseases 60

Types of Plants 62

At a Glance

Aquarium Care When
You Go on Vacation 68

Tetras

Black Widow Tetra
Gymnocorymbus ternetzi

Black widow tetras are a popular aquarium fish. They are calm, long-living, and easy to socialize. They should be in a school of at least six fish. The males are smaller and leaner. Over time, the black coloring may fade a bit. The aquarium should be well planted.

Origin:	Brazil (Mato Grosso), Bolivia
Size:	about 2.5 inches
Tank size:	from about 24 inches, middle water zone
Water:	72–79°F, soft/medium hardness, pH 6–7.5
Food:	complete food, freeze-dried food

Glowlight Tetra
Hemigrammus erythrozonus

Glowlight tetras are calm, peaceful schooling fish. They should be in a school of at least six fish. Glowlight tetras are easy to socialize with other fish. The shining stripes are shown off to best effect in a densely planted tank with dark gravel.

Origin:	Republic of Guyana
Size:	about 2 inches
Tank size:	from about 24 inches, middle water zone
Water:	72–79°F, soft/medium hardness, pH 6–7.5
Food:	complete food, freeze-dried food

Head-and-Taillight Tetra
Hemigrammus ocellifer

Head-and-taillight tetras are peaceful schooling fish. They should be in a school of at least six fish. Head-and-taillight tetras are easy to socialize with other similar fish. They do well in a densely planted tank with dark gravel.

Home:	Amazon
Size:	about 2 inches
Tank size:	from about 24 inches, middle water zone
Water:	75–82°F, soft/medium hardness, pH 6–7.5
Food:	complete food, freeze-dried food

Pretty Tetra
Hemigrammus pulcher

Pretty tetras should be in a school of at least six fish. Plant the boundaries of the aquarium with dense foliage, floating plants, and roots to show off their bright colors. They require plenty of space to swim and dark gravel.

Origin:	West Amazon
Size:	about 2 inches
Tank size:	from about 24 inches, middle water zone
Water:	75–82°F, soft/medium hardness, pH 6–7.2
Food:	complete food, freeze-dried food

Ornate Tetra
Hyphessobrycon bentosi bentosi

Ornate tetras feel most at home with other peaceful fish. They should be in a school of at least six fish, and couples are ideal. A densely planted tank with dark gravel will show off the wonderful colors of this fish.

Origin:	Republic of Guyana
Size:	about 2–3 inches
Tank size:	from about 24 inches, middle water zone
Water:	75–82°F, soft/medium hardness, pH 6–7.5
Food:	complete food, freeze-dried food

Flame Tetra
Hyphessobrycon flammeus

These fish are easy to socialize with other peaceful fish and should be in a school of at least six fish. They thrive in a well-planted tank (background and sides) with dark gravel.

Origin:	Brazil (outskirts of Rio de Janeiro)
Size:	about 1.5 inches
Tank size:	from about 20 inches, middle water zone.
Water:	68–79°F, soft/medium hardness, pH 6–7.5
Food:	complete food, freeze-dried food

Black Neon Tetra

Hyphessobrycon herbertaxelrodi

Black neon tetras are ideal for a neon fish tank and best suited with other peaceful species of fish. They school in groups of eight fish or more and need a densely planted tank with a dark substrate. They live in the middle and upper water zones.

Origin:	Amazon basin
Size:	about 1.5 inches
Tank size:	from about 24 inches, middle water zone
Water:	73–81°F, soft, pH 6–7.2
Food:	complete food, freeze-dried food

Lemon Tetra

Hyphessobrycon pulchripinnis

Lemon tetras are suited to a large fish community and thrive in a school of eight or more fish. They require a densely planted aquarium and plenty of space to swim. They live in the middle water zone.

Origin:	Brazil
Size:	about 2 inches
Tank size:	from about 24 inches, middle water zone
Water:	75–79°F, soft/medium hardness, pH 6–7.5
Food:	good quality fish food, mosquito larvae, food tablets

Red Eye Tetra

Moenkhausia sanctaefilomenae

Red eye tetras are easy-to-keep schooling fish (at least six in a school) and easy to socialize. Grow plants along the sides of the tank with plenty of swimming space.

Origin:	Tropical South America
Size:	about 2.5 inches
Tank size:	from about 32 inches, middle water zone
Water:	72–82°F, soft/medium hardness, pH 6–7.5
Food:	complete food, freeze-dried food

Cardinal Tetra
Paracheirodon axelrodi

These lively schooling fish are among the most attractive and popular species. They socialize well with smaller species. They prefer a densely planted tank with plenty of space to swim.

Origin:	Colombia, Venezuela, Brazil
Size:	about 1.5–2 inches
Tank size:	from about 24 inches, middle water zone
Water:	73–77°F, soft, pH 5–7
Food:	complete food, small amounts of live food

Neon Tetra
Paracheirodon innesi

These colorful, peaceful fish prefer a well-planted tank. They are sociable and prefer to live in a shoal of at least ten fish. In contrast to the cardinal tetra, this species breeds in large numbers.

Origin:	Colombia, Peru, Brazil (upper Amazon)
Size:	about 1.5 inches
Tank size:	from about 20 inches, middle water zone
Water:	75–82°F, soft/medium hardness, pH 6–7.5
Food:	complete food, micro-food tablets

False Penguin Tetra
Thayeria boehlkei

Penguin tetras thrive in a shoal of at least six fish and are characterized by their markings and very quick swimming. They mix well with similar tetra species and love loose planting on the edges and plenty of swimming space.

Origin:	tropical South America
Size:	about 3 inches
Tank size:	from about 32 inches, middle to upper water zone
Water:	72–79°F, soft/medium hardness, pH 6–7.5
Food:	complete food, freeze-dried food, freeze-dried insects

Carp

Leopard Danio
Brachydanio frankei

Leopard danios are shoaling fish and should be in a group of at least eight. They are lively and easy to breed. This species has been selectively bred in captivity.

Origin:	Bred in captivity
Size:	about 2 inches
Tank size:	from about 24 inches, middle to upper water zone
Water:	72–79°F, soft/medium hardness, pH 6.5–7.5
Food:	complete nutrition, freeze-dried food

Siamese Algae Eater
Crossocheilus siamensis

Siamese algae eaters work well as "cleaner fish." They thrive in a school of at least six fish. They love densely planted aquariums with smooth stones and plenty of roots.

Origin:	Thailand
Size:	about 4.5–5.5 inches
Tank size:	from about 32 inches, lower water zone
Water:	72–82°F, soft/medium hardness, pH 6.5–7.5
Food:	food tablets and plenty of plants

Giant Danio
Danio aequipinnatus

Giant danios are lively fish that inhabit the upper water zone and do best in a school of at least eight fish. They thrive at the edges of the tank around the plants and need plenty of space to swim.

Origin:	Peninsular India, Sri Lanka
Size:	about 3–4 inches
Tank size:	from about 40 inches, upper water zone
Water:	75–82°F, soft/medium hardness, pH 6.5–7.5
Food:	freeze-dried food and insects

Zebra Fish
Danio rerio

Zebra fish are well-known shoaling fish. Get at least eight fish to start off. They are easily socialized with other fish. They prefer plenty of swimming space and plants at the edges of tank with high growth.

Origin:	India, Pakistan
Size:	about 2 inches
Tank size:	from about 24 inches, middle to upper water zone
Water:	64–79°F, soft/medium hardness, pH 6–7.5
Food:	complete food, freeze-dried food and insects, food tablets

Rosy Barb
Puntius conchonius

Rosy barbs thrive in a shoal of at least six fish and are easy to socialize with other robust fish. They love a well-planted aquarium community with plenty of space to swim.

Origin:	India (Bengal, Assam)
Size:	about 3–4 inches
Tank size:	from about 40 inches, middle to lower water zone
Water:	64–79°F, soft/medium hardness, pH 6.5–7.5
Food:	complete food, freeze-dried food, food tablets

Black Ruby Barb
Puntius nigrofasciatus

These fish socialize well with other species of barbs. They thrive in a shoal of at least seven other fish. They prefer dense plant canopies and long roots of floating plants and are most comfortable with dark gravel.

Origin:	Sri Lanka
Size:	about 3 inches
Tank size:	from about 32 inches, middle to lower water zone
Water:	75–79°F, soft/medium hardness, pH 6–7.5
Food:	complete food

Carp

Checkered Barb
Puntius oligolepis

If they feel comfortable, these shoaling fish, with at least six in a school, display their beautiful copper colors. They prefer plants at the edges and background of the tank, but leave some swimming space for them. Dark gravel is best and roots are used for hiding.

Origin:	Indonesia (Padang, Sumatra)
Size:	about 2 inches
Tank size:	from about 24 inches, middle to lower water zone
Water:	72–79°F, soft/medium hardness, pH 6–7.5
Food:	complete food, freeze-dried food, food tablets

Gold Barb
Puntius semifasciolatus

These vivacious fish, which thrive in a school of at least seven, have an attractive, shimmering gold brocade pattern. They like a well-planted community tank with plenty of plants on the edges and free space to swim.

Origin:	Southeast China
Size:	about 3 inches
Tank size:	from about 32 inches, middle to lower water zone
Water:	64–79°F, soft/medium hardness, pH 6.5–7.5
Food:	complete food, freeze-dried food, food tablets, specialty food

Tiger Barb
Puntius tetrazona

These are very popular fish with aquarium owners. Tiger barbs socialize well with other lively barbs, except long-finned breeds. They thrive in a school of at least six fish. A variation is the beautiful moss green with the same care requirements.

Origin:	Sumatra, Borneo
Size:	about 3 inches
Tank size:	from about 32 inches, middle to lower water zone
Water:	75–79°F, soft/medium hardness, pH 6.5–7.5
Food:	an omnivore with varied dietary needs

Cherry Barb

Puntius titteya

These fish are schooling fish, needing at least six fish, with two males for every three females. They socialize well with other peaceful fish. They thrive in a well-planted tank with plenty of open space, hiding places, and dark gravel.

Origin:	Southeast China
Size:	about 2 inches
Tank size:	from about 24 inches, middle to lower water zone
Water:	72–82°F, soft/ medium hardness, pH 6–7.2
Food:	complete food, food tablets

White Cloud Mountain Minnow

Tanichthys albonubes

This species is one of the oldest aquarium fish. They are extremely popular and lively schooling fish (at least ten in a school) that prefer a lively community aquarium with dense planting at the edges and lots of free swimming space. They are easy to breed.

Origin:	China (Canton)
Size:	about 1.5 inches
Tank size:	from about 20 inches, upper water zone
Water:	61–77°F, soft/ medium hardness, pH 6.5–7.5
Food:	complete food, freeze-dried insects, micro-food

Harlequin Rasbora

Trigonostigma heteromorpha

These fish thrive in a school of at least eight and prefer community aquariums with other peaceful species. They like a densely planted tank and plenty of swimming space.

Origin:	Malay Peninsula, Sumatra
Size:	about 2 inches
Tank size:	from about 24 inches, upper to middle water zone
Water:	73–82°F, soft/ medium hardness, pH 6–7.2
Food:	complete food, freeze-dried food, food tablets

Catfish

Bristle-Nosed Catfish
Ancistrus dolichopterus

They are active at twilight and display interesting behaviors. They require an aquarium with robust plant growth, smooth rocks, and roots as shelter. They graze on algae. Keep a pair together.

Origin:	Amazon basin
Size:	about 4–6 inches
Tank size:	from about 32 inches, lower water zone
Water:	72–79°F, soft, pH 6–7.2
Food:	vegetation, food tablets (if not enough food is provided, the catfish will eat the aquatic plants!)

Bronze Corydoras
Corydoras aeneus

The job of this fish species is to clean and revitalize the gravel on the bottom of the tank. Rounded, fine-grained gravel is necessary. Keep a school of at least five (two males for every three females).

Origin:	Trinidad to Rio de la Plata (South America)
Size:	about 2.5 inches
Tank size:	from about 24 inches, lower water zone
Water:	68–79°F, soft to medium hardness, pH 6–7.5
Food:	special food tablets

Leopard Cory
Corydoras leopardus

These catfish are sociable, easy to care for, and socialize well with peaceful fish. Like all catfish, they need fine gravel to graze in so their barbells are not damaged. They also use gravel to hide in.

Origin:	Eastern Brazil, Ecuador, Peru
Size:	about 3 inches
Tank size:	from about 32 inches, lower water zone
Water:	68–77°F, soft to medium hardness, pH 6–7.5
Food:	complete food, plant-based foods

Peppered Corydoras
Corydoras paleatus

These catfish live well together with other armored catfish in the lower water zone in a community tank. Keep a school of at least five (two males for every three females). Rounded, fine-grained substrate is important.

Origin:	Rio de la Plata (South America)
Size:	about 3 inches
Tank size:	from about 24 inches, lower water zone
Water:	64–79°F, soft/ medium hardness, pH 6–7.5
Food:	food tablets

Chinese Algae Eater
Gyrinocheilus aymonieri

They are very efficient algae eaters when young. The adults tend to fight, so they need to be kept separately, but they socialize with other large fish. They require hollow roots and stones for shelter.

Origin:	Indo-China, Thailand
Size:	about 10 inches
Tank size:	from about 40 inches, lower water zone
Water:	72–82°F, soft/ medium hardness, pH 6–7.5
Food:	food tablets, complete food, plant-based food

Dwarf Suckermouth Catfish
Otocinclus affinis

These are ideal algae eaters and thrive in a school of at least five fish. They socialize well with other peaceful fish. They prefer a well-planted aquarium with plenty of roots and smooth stones.

Origin:	Amazon basin to river mouth
Size:	about 1.5–2 inches
Tank size:	from about 20 inches, lower water zone
Water:	68–82°F, soft/ medium hardness, pH 6–7.5
Food:	food tablets, complete food with plenty of plants

Labyrinth Fish

Siamese Fighting Fish
Betta splendens

Males fight each other; therefore, only keep one male, possibly with two or three females, in a community tank with peaceful fish that do not attack the fins. Keep them in a densely planted tank with plenty of hiding places.

Origin:	Southeast Asia
Size:	about 3 inches
Tank size:	from about 24 inches, upper to middle water zone
Water:	77–86°F, soft/medium hardness, pH 6.5–7.5
Food:	freeze-dried food, mosquito larvae, live food

Dwarf Gourami
Colisa lalia

These fish thrive in a densely planted tank and socialize well with peaceful fish that do not bite their threadlike stomach fins. Several colors are available. The males are significantly larger than the females.

Origin:	India (Assam), Bangladesh
Size:	about 2–2.5 inches
Tank size:	from about 24 inches, upper to middle water zone
Water:	77–86°F, soft/medium hardness, pH 6–7.5
Food:	freeze-dried food, insects, food tablets

Kissing Gourami
Helostoma temminckii

These fish thrive in a community tank with peaceful, robust fish and leafy aquatic plants. Keep one or two pairs. This labyrinth fish does not build a foam nest but spawns in the open water.

Origin:	Malay Peninsula, Sumatra, Borneo
Size:	about 10 inches, some varieties 6 inches
Tank size:	from about 47 inches, middle water zone
Water:	75–86°F, soft/medium hardness, pH 6.5–7.5
Food:	complete food, food tablets

Paradise Fish
Macropodus opercularis

They thrive in a well-planted aquarium with hiding places and socialize well with equal-sized robust fish. Keep one male for every two or three females to begin with. Floating plants are required for shelter. They breed in foam nests.

Origin:	Eastern China
Size:	about 4 inches
Tank size:	from about 32 inches, upper to middle water zone
Water:	64–82°F, soft/ medium hardness, pH 6–8
Food:	mosquito larvae, complete food

Pearl Gourami
Trichogaster leeri

They thrive in a densely planted community tank with other peaceful species. Keep one male for every two females. Floating plants are necessary for shelter and for foam nests.

Origin:	Malaysia, Sumatra, Borneo
Size:	about 4.5 inches
Tank size:	from about 47 inches, upper to middle water zone
Water:	77–84°F, soft to medium hardness, pH 6.5–7.5
Food:	food tablets, freeze-dried insects, complete food, freeze-dried food

Three-Spot Gourami
Trichogaster trichopterus

They thrive in a densely planted community tank with other peaceful species. Keep one male for every two females. Floating plants are necessary for shelter and for foam nests. Also found in marbled or spotted gourami varieties.

Origin:	Southeast Asia
Size:	about 6 inches
Tank size:	from about 40 inches, upper to middle water zone
Water:	77–84°F, soft to medium hardness, pH 6.5–7.5
Food:	food tablets, freeze-dried insects, complete food, freeze-dried food

Live-Bearing Tooth Carp

Dwarf Live-Bearer
Heterandria formosa

These are the ideal beginner fish. They can be kept in almost any tap water. They prefer a densely planted tank with their own species or other small, peaceful fish. Keep one male for every two or three females.

Origin:	Florida, South Carolina
Size:	males about 1 inch, females about 1.25 inches
Tank size:	from about 16 inches, middle water zone
Water:	64–79°F, medium hardness, pH 6.5–7.5
Food:	small solid food, micro-food

Guppy
Poecilia reticulate

These fish can breed prolifically. Provide areas of Java moss for pregnant females to protect the young from being eaten. There are various breeds. They can socialize with peaceful fish. Keep one male for every three females. Many plants are required.

Origin:	Trinidad, Venezuela, northern South America
Size:	males about 1.5–2 inches, females about 2.5 inches
Tank size:	from about 16 inches, middle water zone
Water:	73–79°F, medium hardness, pH 6.5–8
Food:	freeze-dried food, mosquito larvae, micro-food, complete food

Black Molly
Poecilia sphenops

These are popular fish for beginners. They thrive in a densely planted tank. Keep them with peaceful fish, especially other live-bearing species, and have one male for every two or three females. Black mollies graze on algae, and there are many varieties.

Origin:	Central America, Colombia
Size:	about 3 inches
Tank size:	from about 24 inches, middle to upper water zone
Water:	75–82°F, medium hardness, pH 6.5–8
Food:	complete food with plenty of plants, food tablets

Green Swordtail
Xiphophorus helleri

These are popular and peaceful schooling fish that thrive in a well-planted community tank and need plenty of space to swim. Keep one male for every three females. There are many breeds and colors with enlarged fins.

Origin:	Mexico, Central America
Size:	about 4–4.5 inches
Tank size:	from about 32 inches, middle water zone
Water:	73–79°F, medium hardness, pH above 7
Food:	complete food with plenty of plants, specialty food

Southern Platyfish
Xiphophorus maculates

These are attractive and popular fish with many color varieties that thrive in a densely planted community tank but also require plenty of space to swim. Keep one male for every three females. They can be crossbred with other swordtails.

Origin:	Central America, Mexico
Size:	males about 1.5 inches, females about 2.5 inches
Tank size:	from about 24 inches, middle water zone
Water:	73–79°F, medium hardness, pH 6.5–8
Food:	complete food, food tablets, micro-food

Variable Platyfish
Xiphophorus variatus

These are lively schooling fish and algae cleaners that are easy to socialize with other species. Keep one male for every two or three females. They are bred in many different colors.

Origin:	Central America, Mexico
Size:	about 2.5–3 inches
Tank size:	from about 24 inches, middle to upper water zone
Water:	72–77°F, medium hardness, pH 6–8
Food:	complete food, food tablets, micro-food

Killifish, Halfbeaks

Golden Wonder Killifish

Aplocheilus lineatus

These fish enjoy spending time swimming between floating plants and are easy to breed. Keep one male for every two or three females. They socialize well with similar-sized, peaceful species of fish.

Origin:	India, Sri Lanka
Size:	about 4 inches
Tank size:	from about 32 inches, middle to upper water zone
Water:	72–82°F, medium hardness, pH 6–7.5
Food:	complete food, freeze-dried insects, floating food, small fish

Blue Panchax

Aplocheilus panchax

These fish enjoy spending time among floating plant roots. Keep one male for every two or three females. They are easy to breed and can socialize with similar large, peaceful species of fish.

Origin:	Sri Lanka, Thailand, Malaysia, Indonesia
Size:	about 3 inches
Tank size:	from about 24 inches, upper water zone
Water:	68–79°F, soft to medium hardness, pH 6–7.5
Food:	complete food, freeze-dried insects, floating food, small fish

Wrestling Halfbeak

Dermogenys pusillus

These live-bearing fish live in the upper water zone and thrive in a school of at least six fish. They are best suited with same-sized fish species. Floating plants are needed.

Origin:	Southeast Asia
Size:	about 2.5–3 inches
Tank size:	from about 24 inches, upper water zone
Water:	75–82°F, soft to medium hardness, pH 6.5–7.5
Food:	good quality food pellets, mosquito larvae, small amount of freeze-dried insects, vitamin-rich dried food

Cichlids

African Butterfly Cichlid
Anomalochromis thomasi

They thrive in a well-planted tank with roots and smooth rocks. Keep one or two pairs together and socialize them with other peaceful fish.

Origin: West Africa

Size: about 3–4 inches

Tank size: from about 32 inches, lower to middle water zone

Water: 75–82°F, soft to medium hardness, pH 6–7.5

Food: complete food, freeze-dried insects, freeze-dried food

Agassiz's Dwarf Cichlid
Apistogramma agassizii

They thrive in a well-planted tank with rock crevices and root wood. Keep one or two pairs together and socialize them with other peaceful fish. There are some color variations.

Origin: upper and mid-Amazon

Size: about 3 inches

Tank size: from about 32 inches, lower water zone

Water: 75–82°F, soft to medium hardness, pH 5.5–7.2

Food: vitamin-enriched freeze-dried food, live food

Keyhole Cichlid
Cleithracara maronii

A couple of peaceful cichlids are suited to a well-planted community tank with other peaceful fish species. They hide among roots and stones.

Origin: Guyana

Size: about 4.5 inches

Tank size: from about 40 inches, lower water zone

Water: 75–82°F, soft to medium hardness, pH 6–7.5

Food: complete food, freeze-dried food, freeze-dried insects

Cichlids

Dwarf Flag Cichlid
Laetacara curviceps

They thrive in densely planted aquariums with plenty of stones and roots. They socialize well with other peaceful fish in the middle and upper water zones, when dense vegetation and many hiding places are present. Keep one or two pairs.

Origin: Amazon basin
Size: about 3 inches
Tank size: from about 24 inches, middle to lower water zone
Water: 72–79°F, soft to medium hardness, pH 6–7.5
Food: complete food, freeze-dried food, live food

Ram Cichlid
Microgeophagus (Papiliochromis) ramirezi

These fish thrive in densely planted aquariums with plenty of stones and roots. They socialize well with other peaceful fish in the middle and upper water zones, when dense vegetation and many hiding places are present. Keep one or two pairs.

Origin: Colombia, Venezuela
Size: about 2.5 inches
Tank size: from about 24 inches, middle to lower water zone, add peat to water
Water: 75–86°F, soft, pH 5–7
Food: complete food, freeze-dried food, live food, mosquito larvae

Golden Dwarf Cichlid
Nannacara anomala

They thrive in densely planted aquariums with plenty of stones and roots. They socialize well with other peaceful fish in the middle and upper water zones, when dense vegetation and many hiding places are present. Keep one or two pairs. They will usually spawn, and the female will defend the territory and her young.

Origin: Guyana
Size: about 3.5 inches
Tank size: from about 24 inches, middle to lower water zone
Water: 75–82°F, medium to hard, pH 6–7.5
Food: complete food, vitamin-enriched freeze-dried food, food tablets

Kribensis
Pelvicachromis pulcher

These fish thrive in densely planted aquariums with plenty of stones and roots. They socialize well in a community aquarium when dense vegetation and many hiding places are present. Keep one or two pairs. This species requires a swimming area of at least 23.5 inches.

Origin:	West Africa
Size:	about 3–4 inches
Tank size:	from about 32 inches, lower water zone, filter water through peat
Water:	75–82°F, soft/medium hardness, pH 6–7.5
Food:	freeze-dried food, food tablets, specialty food

Egyptian Mouthbrooder
Pseudocrenilabrus multicolor

They thrive with other peaceful species of fish. Keep one male for every two females. The female mouthbrooder cares for the offspring.

Origin:	North Africa to Tanzania
Size:	about 3 inches
Tank size:	from about 24 inches, lower to middle water zone
Water:	73–81°F, medium hardness, pH 7–8
Food:	freeze-dried food, complete food

Angelfish
Pterophyllum scalare

Angelfish thrive in aquariums with plants at the back and sides and in a school of at least five or six fish. They socialize with medium-sized peaceful fish. (They will eat smaller fish.) There are several different kinds to choose from, including black, golden, marble, smoke, and veil.

Origin:	Amazon basin
Size:	about 6–10 inches
Tank size:	from about 40 inches, middle water zone, water filtered through peat
Water:	75–82°F, soft/medium hardness, pH 5–7.5
Food:	vitamin-enriched freeze-dried food, food tablets, mosquito larvae

Cichlids

Firemouth Cichlid

Thorichthys meeki

These fish prefer aquariums with round stones and rocks, wood and roots, and plenty of plants at the edges. They can be socialized with other cichlids and larger fish species. They need to be in a school of at least four to six fish, in pairs. The females are smaller and not as brightly colored.

Origin: Central America
Size: about 4.5–6 inches
Tank size: from about 40 inches, lower water zone
Water: 72–82°F, medium hardness, pH 7–8
Food: food tablets, mosquito larvae, good-quality food from pet shop

Tanganyikan Cichlid
(Golden Julie)

Julidochromis ornatus

They thrive in a school of fish and need to be in an aquarium with plenty of rocks with crevices and holes, ribbonlike plants, and sandy gravel (a grain size of 1 to 2 millimeters).

Origin: Lake Tanganyika (Africa)
Size: about 3 inches
Tank size: from about 24 inches, lower to middle water zone
Water: 75–81°F, hard water, pH 7.5–8.5
Food: food tablets, complete food, freeze-dried food

Princess of Burundi

Neolamprologus brichardi

These fish thrive in a school of fish with four to six members. They need plenty of rocks with crevices and holes, ribbonlike plants, and sandy gravel (a grain size of 1 to 2 millimeters).

Origin: Lake Tanganyika (Africa)
Size: about 3 inches
Tank size: from about 32 inches, lower to middle water zone
Water: 75–81°F, hard water, pH 7.5–8.5
Food: food tablets, complete food, freeze-dried food

Lemon Cichlid
Neolamprologus leleupi

This brightly colored, attractive species of fish is easy to socialize with other species. It requires the same tank setup as the previous two fish.

Origin:	Lake Tanganyika (Africa)
Size:	about 3 inches
Tank size:	from about 32 inches, lower to middle water zone
Water:	75–81°F, hard water, pH 7.5–8.5
Food:	food tablets, complete food, freeze-dried food

Electric Blue Johanni
Melanochromis johannii

This species requires the same tank setup as with the previously mentioned fish species and can easily be socialized with other Lake Malawi cichlids of equal size. Keep one male (electric blue) for every three females (yellow).

Origin:	Lake Malawi (Africa)
Size:	about 4–4.5 inches
Tank size:	from at least about 40 inches, lower to middle water zone
Water:	75–82°F, hard water, pH 7.5–8.5
Food:	food tablets, plenty of plants

Auratus Cichlid
Melanochro mis auratus

The male is black with blue stripes; the female is yellow with black stripes. These fish need a tank with plenty of hiding places (rock structures with holes and columns), plenty of plants at the edges of the tank, and sandy gravel (a grain size of 1 to 2 millimeters). Keep one male for every three females. Auratus cichlids can be socialized with other Lake Malawi cichlids.

Origin:	Lake Malawi (Africa)
Size:	about 4.5 inches
Tank size:	from at least about 40 inches, lower to middle water zone
Water:	75–82°F, hard water, pH 7.5–8.5
Food:	food tablets, plenty of plants

→ The Most Common Fish Diseases

Problem	Cause	Solution
white spots on body of fish, limp fins, lethargy, loss of appetite, rubbing against objects	the parasite *Ichthyophthirius multifiliis*	Purchase medication to get rid of the parasite. Follow dosage instructions very carefully until all the white spots have gone.
velvety-gray patches on the skin, limp fins, lethargy, loss of appetite, rubbing against objects, skin and fins disintegrate, infestation in gills, gasping for air	*Oodinium pillularis* (similar to above parasite)	Purchase medication to get rid of the parasite. Follow dosage instructions very carefully.
gray, scaly patches on the skin and fins, rubbing against objects, skin and fins slowly disintegrate	such parasites as *Costia, Chilodonella, Trichodina, Trichodinella, Tripartiella, Tetrahymena*	Purchase medication to get rid of the parasite. Follow dosage instructions very carefully. Change one-third of the water in the tank. During treatment, use a cotton wool filter. After the water change, use an activated carbon filter.
moldy-looking areas around wounds on mouth and fins	*Saprolegnia* infecting wounds and skin tears	Buy an antifungal remedy from a pet shop. Identify the cause of the wounds, such as sharp gravel, other fish, or poor water conditions.
fish not eating well	ailments poor water conditions wrong food	Check water levels and improve them if necessary. Use high-quality food. Use medication for parasites.

Problem	Cause	Solution
fish breathe very fast, float on the surface, try to jump out of the tank, jerk as they swim, twitch, have inflamed gills	lack of oxygen sudden shock in new water alkali or acid damage poisoning	Oxygenate the water. Check the temperature and that the tank equipment is working properly. → If the water is too alkaline (pH about 8.5), it requires a partial water change; add peat extract, peat filters, water treatments. → If the water is too acidic (pH below 5.5), do a partial water change with buffered water (buffer solutions are available from pet shops) on gravel or through the filter. → If it is due to ammonia or nitrite poisoning, acidify water to pH 6.7 (with treatment from pet shop). Test the pH and KH values. → In case of poisoning by pesticides, insect sprays, or household goods, do a partial water change, use water-treatment products, use a carbon filter, and provide strong aeration. → For chlorine poisoning, partly change the water, aeration, or surface movement.
fish dying without any obvious symptoms	poisoning	Find out the cause (you may need to ask a vet) and use necessary treatment.
fish swimming to water's surface, breathing very quickly	lack of oxygen	Ensure plenty of water movement. Ventilation may be required. Check the temperature. Remove any sludge, dirt, or old filter material. Determine whether there are too many fish in the tank. Labyrinth fish require airspace between water surface and the tank cover.
fish rub themselves against objects in the tank, have wilted fins, poor appetite, poor swimming	parasites damage from poor water conditions	Buy medication for parasites. Do a partial water change.
eyes bulging	poor water conditions	Do a partial water change. Measure water levels and make necessary changes.

Anubias Minima
Anubias barteri var. glabra

This plant is from West Africa. Plant it in the foreground, leaving stems uncovered, or tie it onto rocks and roots with nylon. It grows slowly but well. Use peat filter and fertilizer. Water hardness should be soft to medium, 72–79 °F.

Dwarf Anubias
Anubias barteri var. nana

An adaptable plant, it grows slowly but strongly and makes attractive nests for fish. It is suitable for the foreground or tied to roots or stones. Water hardness should be soft to medium, 72–79 °F.

Wavy-Edged Aponogeton
Aponogeton crispus

This ideal beginner plant is from South India and Sri Lanka. Buds on tubers should remain uncovered. After two to three vegetation periods, keep tubers for six to eight weeks in a cool and airy place. Water hardness should be soft to medium, 77–86°F.

Giant Red Bacopa
Bacopa caroliniana

This attractive plant is from southeast North America. Plant it in middle and edges of the tank in groups of five to ten. Cut 2 inches from the stem ends, remove leaves at the base, and plant it about 1.5 inches deep into the substrate. Water hardness should be soft to medium, 68–79°F.

African Water Fern
Bolbitis heudelotii

This tropical fern plant is from Africa. It grows on decorative wood roots and stones and likes to grow in the filter current. It requires low to moderate lighting and soft water, pH 5–6.9, 72–82°F.

Green Cabomba
Cabomba caroliniana

This is a light-hungry, fast-growing plant from North America. Plant ten to fifteen in the middle ground and on the sides of the tank. If the plants are too long, shorten the shoots and replant. Use peat filters, plant food, fertilizer, and as much CO_2 as possible. It can live in either soft or hard water, 73–77°F.

Red Cabomba
Cabomba furcata

It is from Central and South America. It looks good In a group in the middle and background of the tank. It is a little sensitive but fast-growing plant that needs a lot of light and soft water, pH-neutral to acidic, 75–86°F.

Red-Brown Cabomba
Cabomba palaeformis

It is from Central America and needs moderate lighting. It reproduces from side shoots and comes in green and reddish-brown varieties. Place it in the background in a group in medium-hard water, 68–82°F.

Coon's Tail
Ceratophyllum demersum

This is a vigorous, highly recommended plant that grows in many parts of the world. It removes pollutants from water, can be grown in small groups, and is useful to fish for hiding or spawning in and also as a territorial boundary. It needs hard water, 72–82°F.

Water Sprite
Ceratopteris thalictroides

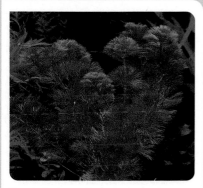

This plant is widespread in the tropics and can be rooted or free floating. It is ideal for labyrinth fish foam nests. Put the plants at the edges of large tanks. They need soft to medium water hardness, 72–82°F.

Crypt Affinis
Cryptocoryne affinis

This aquarium plant from the Malay Peninsula is used by harlequin fish as a spawning substrate. Place plants at the sides and background. There are many different types. They require moderate/high lighting and medium water hardness, 72–79°F.

Water Trumpet
Cryptocoryne albida

From southern Thailand, this plant has green and reddish brown variations and grows in the foreground with a good light source. It thrives in small groups in low to moderate lighting and soft/medium water, 75–82°F.

Cryptocoryne Aponogetifolia
Cryptocoryne aponogetifolia

This plant is for large aquariums, especially cichlid tanks. The foliage is striking, slow growing, and forms spurs. Use it in the background and sides of the tank. It has low lighting requirements and needs medium/hard water, 72–81°F.

Crypt Beckettii
Cryptocoryne beckettii

From Sri Lanka, this undemanding plant is suitable for most types of water. It looks especially nice in front of bright green background plants. It needs low to moderate lighting and soft/medium water, 72–79°F.

Crypt Undulata
Cryptocoryne undulata

This plant is from Sri Lanka and has attractive dark brown, usually mottled leaves. Plant small groups together in the aquarium. They require low/moderate lighting and soft/medium water, 72–79°F.

Crypt Wendtii
Cryptocoryne wendtii

This fast-growing plant from Sri Lanka is ideal for a start-up aquarium. Plant it in the front and center in a slightly shady area among other plants. It needs regular partial water changes, iron and fertilizer, pH 5–8, and soft/medium water, 72–79°F.

Lucens
Cryptocoryne x willisii

From Sri Lanka, this plant grows slowly in the foreground of the aquarium and then grows quicker once it reaches the surface. It has moderate light requirements and needs soft/medium, water 72–79°F.

Amazon Sword Plant
Echinodorus amazonicus

This plant comes from the Amazon and needs soft/medium water, 72–79°F.

Radican Sword
Echinodorus cordifolius
This plant comes from southeast North America and Venezuela. Use it as a center-piece in a large aquarium. It needs a great amount of light, a nutritious substrate, and medium/hard water, 68–82°F.

Dwarf Sword
Echinodorus parviflorus
This popular, very vigorous plant from South America grows about 10 to 12 inches high. This bright green plant is good for middle and front areas and needs a nutritious substrate, good fertilizer, and soft/medium water, 72–82°F.

Pigmy Chain Sword
Echinodorus tenellus
Farm-raised in the United States, this plant needs moderate lighting and soft/medium water, 64–79°F. Do not use it in a tank with burrowing, plant-eating fish!

Brazilian Elodea
Egeria densa
This fast-growing plant comes from Brazil, Argentina, and Uruguay. Shorten the stem ends slightly by 2 inches and plant them about 1.5 inches into the gravel. It will reach the surface of water and needs soft water, 50–79°F.

Brazilian Pennywort
Hydrocotyle leucocephala
This particularly fast-growing and decorative plant comes from Central and South America. It improves water quality by consuming nitrogen. If the shoots are too long, shorten them and replant. It needs soft water, 68–82°F.

Temple Plant
Hygrophila corymbosa
This fast-growing plant from Southeast Asia has large leaves and would look beautiful in the center of the tank or in the background with red-leafed plants. Plant them in groups of five, varying in length, 1.5 to 2 inches deep. Plant in medium/hard water, 72–82°F.

Water Wisteria
Hygrophila difformis

This attractive, vigorously growing plant from India to Malaya should be kept in groups of five to ten with lots of light, CO_2, regular water-treatment products, and peat extract. Keep it in soft water, 72–82°F.

Dwarf Hygrophila
Hygrophila polysperma

This fast-growing plant from Southeast Asia looks good in the background, sides, and center of the tank and beautiful in front of darker plants. It has moderate light requirements and grows toward light. Plant it in soft water, 72–82°F.

Brazilian Micro Sword
Lilaeopsis brasiliensis

Also known as New Zealand grass, this plant is slow growing and lawnlike. Put it in front of the brightest place in the aquarium. It needs regular fertilization, moderate lighting, and soft water, 68–79°F.

Asian Ambulia
Limnophila sessiliflora

This stocky, strong plant grows well with lots of light and regular fertilization. Above water, shoots can bloom. Put it at the sides and background of the tank in soft/medium water, 68–79°F.

Cardinal Flower
Lobelia cardinalis

This slow-growing plant is from North America. Grow it in a group in the foreground and middle ground, arranging the plant cuttings in a graduated height. The light requirements are moderate/high, and the water should be medium/hard, 72–79°F.

Java Fern
Microsorum pteropus

Because the roots of this Southeast Asian fern are slightly limp, you will need to bind them with fishing line to wood, stone, or cork. It reproduces from rhizomes and leaves. It needs soft water, 68–82°F.

Rotala Rotundifolia
Rotala rotundifolia

In contrast to the name, this Southeast Asian plant's leaves are narrow and delicate. Grow it in groups of ten to fifteen in the central region of the tank next to round-leaved plants. The cuttings can be planted. It needs lots of light, fertilizer, and soft/medium water, 75–82°F.

Delta Arrowhead
Sagittaria platyphylla

This North American plant has attractive, slender to large, round leaves and is good for the middle area of the tank. It needs lots of light, nutrient-rich soil for the roots, and soft/medium water, 64–82°F.

Dwarf Sagittaria
Sagittaria subulata

This small, lawnlike foreground plant is easy to cultivate and easy to reproduce. When first planting, plant it in groups of ten to fifteen at a distance of about half an inch apart. Plant it in medium/hard water, 64–82°F.

Mexican Oak
Shinnersia rivularis

This very vigorous, undemanding plant from Central America is suited to large aquariums. Regularly thin it out and replant. The light requirements are moderate/high. Plant it in soft water, 68–82°F.

Straight Vallisneria
Vallisneria spiralis

This plant is from the tropics and subtropics. Trim the roots to about 1.25 inches perpendicular to the plant. The leaves should remain uncovered. This plant is fast growing in nutrient-rich ground and medium/hard water, 68–82°F.

Singapore Moss
Vesicularia dubyana

From Asia, this plant grows on wood, lava stone, etc., in tight wads (suitable for baby fish to hide in). Seaweed can inhibit the growth. Plant it in soft water, 64–82°F.

Aquarium Care When You Go on Vacation

Preparations

You will need to make the following preparations before you go on vacation. Do not introduce any new fish in your tank fewer than three weeks before you leave.

→ Five days before you go, clean the filter pump head and replace dirty filter material.

→ Use a bacteria preparation.

→ Check that all the technical devices are working properly.

→ Three days before you go, change one-third of the water and add water treatment.

→ Set the timer so that the lighting goes on at 2 P.M. and goes off at 10 P.M.

Feeding Your Fish

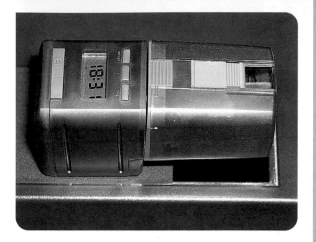

→ A few days of fasting will do your fish no harm.

→ If you will be gone for more than two weeks, use an automatic feeder. Use half the normal amount of food for a daily ration and set the automatic feeder up a few days before you go so you can see whether it works.

→ If friends or family are going to feed your fish while you are away, set out the daily rations for them. If fish are given too much food, this will affect the condition of the water.

Information for the Fish-Sitter

→ Leave written instructions on the temperature and devices, how to check them, and what to do in an emergency.

→ Leave the address and telephone number of your vet and an emergency number where you can be reached if necessary.

Translated from the German edition by Claire Mullen.

Edited and produced by Enslow Publishers, Inc.

Originally published in German.

© 2007 Franckh-Kosmos Verlags-GmbH & Co. KG, Stuttgart, Germany
   Angela Beck, *Aquarium*

Library of Congress Cataloging-in-Publication Data

Beck, Angela.
   [Aquarium. English]
   Fish : keeping and caring for your pet / Angela Beck.
      pages cm. — (Keeping and caring for your pet)
   Includes bibliographical references and index.
   Summary: "Discusses how to choose and care for fish, including diet, behaviors, tank requirements, and profiles on different species of fish and aquatic plants"—Provided by publisher.
   ISBN 978-0-7660-4185-1
   1. Aquarium fishes—Juvenile literature. I. Title.
   SF457.25.B32 2013
   639.8—dc23

                         2012045848

Paperback ISBN 978-1-4644-0301-9

Printed in the United States of America

052013 Lake Book Manufacturing, Inc., Melrose Park, IL

10 9 8 7 6 5 4 3 2 1

To Our Readers: We have done our best to make sure all Internet addresses in this book were active and appropriate when we went to press. However, the author and publisher have no control over and assume no liability for the material available on those Internet sites or on other Web sites they may link to. Any comments or suggestions can be sent by e-mail to comments@enslow.com or to the address on the back cover.

Every effort has been made to locate all copyright holders of material used in this book. If any errors or omissions have occurred, corrections will be made in future editions of this book.

All information in this book is given to the best of the author's knowledge. However, care during implementation is still required. The publishers, authors, and translators assume no liability for personal injury, property damage, or financial loss as a result of the application of the methods and ideas presented in this book.

♻ Enslow Publishers, Inc., is committed to printing our books on recycled paper. The paper in every book contains 10% to 30% post-consumer waste (PCW). The cover board on the outside of each book contains 100% PCW. Our goal is to do our part to help young people and the environment too!

Photo Credits: Color photos by Burkard Kahl, except Peter Beck, pp. 8 (bottom), 9, 11 (top), 13, 14 (bottom), 15, 17, 24 (bottom), 25, 26 (bottom), 27 (middle), 28 (bottom), 29, 30 (bottom), 33; Christel Kasselmann, pp. 62–67; Christof Salata/KOSMOS, p. 11 (bottom); Shutterstock, p. 1.

Cover Photos: *Main photo:* Ameng Wu/Photos.com (Siamese fighting fish). *Bottom, left to right:* Shutterstock.com (dwarf gourami, kribensis, neon tetra, tiger barb). *Back:* Burkard Kahl (author photo); Shutterstock.com (leopard cory).

Index

A

African butterfly cichlid, 55
African water fern, 62
Agassiz's dwarf cichlid, 55
algae, 10, 18, 21, 26, 28, 35, 48, 52, 53
Amazon, 8, 40, 41, 42, 43, 48, 49, 55, 56, 57, 64
Amazon sword plant, 64
angelfish, 57
Anubias minima, 28, 62
Asian ambulia, 66
Auratus cichlid, 59

B

background (decoration), 10, 14
bacteria, 10, 12, 16, 18, 21, 27, 34, 37, 68
black molly, 52
black neon tetra, 42
black ruby barb, 45
black widow tetra, 40
bloodworms, 32
blue panchax, 54
Brazilian elodea, 65
Brazilian micro sword, 66
Brazilian pennywort, 65
bristle-nosed catfish, 35, 48
bronze corydoras, 48

C

carbonate hardness, 19, 21, 25, 29
cardinal flower, 66
cardinal tetra, 43
care plan, 20–21
carp, 44–47
catfish, 15, 30, 33, 35, 36, 48–49
checkered barb, 46
chemistry, 8, 13, 24–25
cherry barb, 47
Chinese algae eater, 49
cichlids, 25, 54–59, 64
conservation, 9
coon's tail, 63
CO$_2$ permanent test, 10, 16, 20, 21, 25
Crypt affinis, 63
Crypt beckettii, 64
Cryptocoryne aponogetifolia, 64
Crypt undulata, 64
Crypt wendtii, 64

D

decorations, 10, 11, 15, 19
delta arrowhead, 67
diseases, 60–61
dwarf anubias, 28, 62
dwarf flag cichlid, 56
dwarf gourami, 50
dwarf hygrophila, 66
dwarf live-bearer, 52
dwarf sagittaria, 67
dwarf suckermouth catfish, 30, 35, 49
dwarf sword, 65

E

Egyptian mouthbrooder, 57
electric blue johanni, 59
equipment, 10, 11, 12–13, 15, 20, 61

F

false penguin tetra, 43
feeding, 20, 32–33, 37, 69
fertilizer, 10, 15, 18, 19, 20, 21, 29, 34, 35, 37, 57, 60, 61, 62, 64, 65, 66, 67
filter, 10, 11, 12–13, 15, 16, 17, 26, 27, 37, 68
firemouth cichlid, 58
fish diseases, 60–61
flame tetra, 41
frogs, 31

G

general hardness, 16, 19, 24, 25, 29
giant danio, 44
giant red bacopa, 62
glowlight tetra, 40
gold barb, 46
golden dwarf cichlid, 56
golden wonder killifish, 54
green cabomba, 62
green swordtail, 53
guppy, 52

H

habitat, 8–9, 14, 15, 16, 24, 28, 32
halfbeaks, 54
harlequin barb, 47
head-and-taillight tetra, 40
heating, 10, 11, 13, 16
hiding, 15, 28, 33, 46, 47, 48, 50, 51, 55, 56, 57, 59, 63, 67

J

Java fern, 66

K

keyhole cichlid, 55
killifish, 54
kissing gourami, 50
Kribensis, 57

L

labyrinth fish, 50–51
lemon cichlid, 59
lemon tetra, 42
leopard cory, 48
leopard danio, 44
lighting, 8, 10, 13, 16, 26, 29, 33, 34, 35, 37, 68
live-bearing tooth carp, 52–53
location (of tank), 10
lucens, 64

M

magnesium, 24
Malawi (Lake), 8, 15, 25, 59
Mexican oak, 67
midge, 33
mosquito larvae, 33

N

neon tetra, 43
nitrate, nitrite, 10, 16, 18, 21, 27, 28, 29, 34, 35

O

oak leaf, 67
ornate tetra, 41
oxygen, 13, 26–27, 28, 36, 37, 61

P

paradise fish, 51
parasites, 33, 60, 61
pearl gourami, 51
peppered corydora, 49
pH value, 8, 10, 16, 19, 21, 25, 29, 35, 37
pigmy chain sword, 65
plant diseases, 34–35
plants, 28–29, 62–67
pretty tetra, 41
princess of Burundi, 58
problems, 18–19, 34–35

R

radican sword, 65
ram cichlid, 56
red-brown cabomba, 63
red cobomba, 63
red eye tetra, 42
roots 10, 15, 18, 28, 29, 41, 44, 45, 46, 48, 49, 54, 55, 56, 57, 58, 62, 63, 66, 67
rosy barb, 45
Rotala rotundifolia, 67

S

safety test, 16–17
shrimp, 31, 33
Siamese algae eater, 35, 44
Siamese fighting fish, 30, 50
Singapore moss, 67
snails, 18, 19, 26, 31, 33, 34
socialization, 30, 40, 41, 42, 43, 45, 46, 47, 48, 49, 50, 51, 52, 53, 54, 55, 56, 57, 58, 59
southern platyfish, 53
stones, 15, 44, 49, 55, 56, 57, 58, 62, 66, 67
straight vallisneria, 67
substrate, 12, 15, 18, 28, 42, 49, 62, 63, 65

T

Tanganyika (Lake), 8, 15, 25, 58, 59
Tanganyikan cichlid, 58
tank size, 11
temperature, 8, 11, 24, 26, 29, 30, 37, 61, 69
temple plant, 65
tetras, 40–43
three-spot gourami, 51
tiger barb, 46

V

vacation, 68–69
variable platyfish, 53
ventilation, 13, 26, 61

W

water fleas, 32
water sprite, 63
water trumpet, 63
water wisteria, 66
wavy-edged aponogeton, 62
white cloud mountain minnow, 47
wrestling halfbeak, 54

Z

zebra fish, 45

Further Reading

Books

Boruchowitz, David E. *The Simple Guide to Freshwater Aquariums.* Neptune City, N.J.: TFH Publications, 2009.

Fletcher, Nick. *What Fish? A Buyer's Guide to Tropical Fish.* Hauppauge, N.Y.: Barron's Educational Series, 2006.

Helfman, Gene, and Bruce Collette. *Fishes: The Animal Answer Guide.* Baltimore: John Hopkins University Press, 2011.

Internet Addresses

ASPCA: Fish Care
http://www.aspca.org/pet-care/small-pet-care/fish-care.aspx

Animal Planet: Aquarium Fish
http://animal.discovery.com/pets/aquarium-fish-care.htm

FishChannel.com
http://www.fishchannel.com